MASTERING KINDLE DIRECT PUBLISHING WITH EASE

Olufemi Felix Iyiola

Copyright © 2021 O. F. Iyiola

ISBN: 9798734426432

Dedicated to the Glory og God Almighty

CONTENTS

FOREWORD

This is a practical step-by-step guide to become self-publisher on Amazon website

PROLOGUE

Lorem ipsum dolor sit amet, consectetur adipiscing elit, sed do
eiusmod tempor incididunt ut labore et dolore magna aliqua. Ut
enim ad minim veniam, quis nostrud exercitation ullamco la-
boris.

INTRODUCTION

This book is intended to teach you practical step-by-step procedure to publish your books on Amazon using Kindle Direct Publishing (KDP) software application tools. The training is divided into two sections, section A for basic training while section B is advanced training. The complete training has been prepared for people such as authors, publishers, teachers, religious leaders, university lecturers, professionals, etc. to publish their work for people across the globe to tap from their wealth of experience. This will give them more recognition across the globe and they can make a lot of money for selling their books on Amazon.

BASIC TRAINING

Basic training involves signing up on Amazon webpage to publish manuscripts of your books. If you have an existing account with Amazon, you just need to log in with your account details. For this training, you will need the following items:

     i.   A laptop/desktop
    ii.   Internet connection (wifi)
   iii.   Stable power supply

Using the computer system web browser, type https://kdp.amazon.com/en_US/ to get to Amazon webpage

Figure 1: Amazon webpage

Click "Sign In" if you have an existing KDP account and supply your e-mail address with password to log in.

Click "Sign Up" if you are a new user, supply your e-mail address and password you intend to use for the KDP account. Follow the onscreen instruction until the account is successfully created.

Click "Your Account" at the top right of the main menu and fill in the following:

 i. Your full name
 ii. Address
 iii. Postal Code
 iv. Phone number
 v. Tax information and click "Save"

The KDP account has four (4) categories which are described below (figure 2):

 i. Bookshelf: This option is required to format the manuscript of the books created in Microsoft word for publishing as e-book or/and paperback
 ii. Reports: Summary of the e-books and paperbacks ordered and shipped is given under this section
 iii. Community: This gives information on new and

accomplished authors and publishers who are using KDP for their work

iv. Marketing: This can be used to promote publishers' work to earn more money and gain more recognition.

Figure 2: KDP main menu

Basic Training for Book Publishing

Click "Bookshelf" on top of the main account where publisher will be able to upload the manuscript of his book for formatting, create book cover and get ISBN. This book can be published as e-book or paperback (figure 3).

Figure 3: Bookshelf to create and format manuscript

Creating e-book

Click "Kindle ebook" to start the process of creating e-books in KDP, the process involves three stages as follows:

    i. Kindle ebook details: This is the stage where publisher will specify the following:

a. Language: Select English for the book, if the manuscript has been written in another language, choose the language from the list of language in the menu

b. Book tittle and sub-tittle if available: Type the book title and its subtitle if necessary

c. Book series: Add series details if the book is part of a series

d. Edition number: Add edition number in digits such as 1,2,3 …

e. Primary author: Add full name of the main author of the book

f. Other contributors: There is provision to add other authors to the book

g. Book description: Description of the book is very important and this will enable readers to have insights of the book to decide that the book is relevant to their work.

h. Publishing right: This describes your publishing right to the contents of the book. It can be individual right or public domain work

i. Keywords: Add major keywords in the book as this will enable readers to easily locate the book in the search engines

j. Categories: This is where users can easily find the book on Amazon site. You can select maximum of two categories in the list

k. Age range: For children books you need to select minimum and maximum age range the books are meant for.

After filling the relevant sections, save the content and continue to the next stage.

ii. Kindle eBook Content: This section is to load the manuscript of the book prepared in Microsoft word and to create cover for the book.

a. Digital Right Management (DRM): This addresses author's permission either to or not to allow unauthorised distribution of their work

b. Upload eBook Manuscript: Click this option and navigate to project folder on the computer system where the manuscript is saved. Load the manuscript

c. Kindle eBook Cover: launch cover creator to create book cover. You can select any suitable cover template from Amazon gallery and use or upload a cover already created by you.

When the manuscript and cover are uploaded successfully, the kindle interface will look like this:

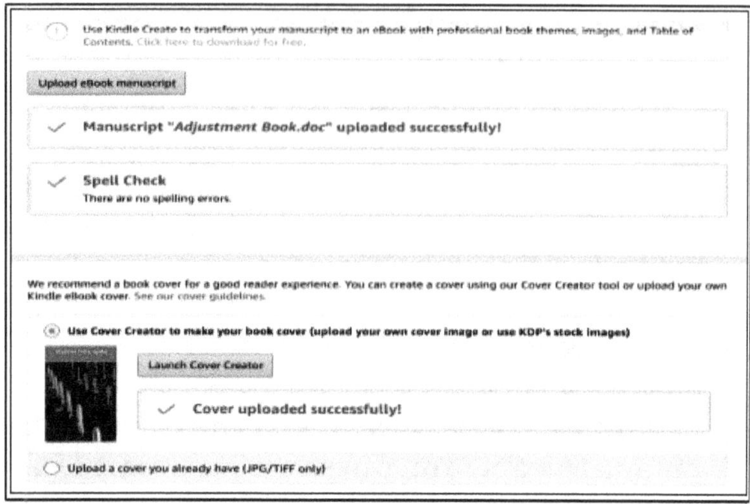

Figure 4: Uploading manuscript and cover in Kindle

Save the page and continue to the next section

      iii.   Kindle eBook Pricing: This deals with setting price for the eBook and royalty on the book including book lending process.

When all the book preparation is satisfactory to the publisher, then, click "Publish Your Kindle eBook" (figure 5). It takes maximum of 72 hours for books to be available for purchase on Amazon site.

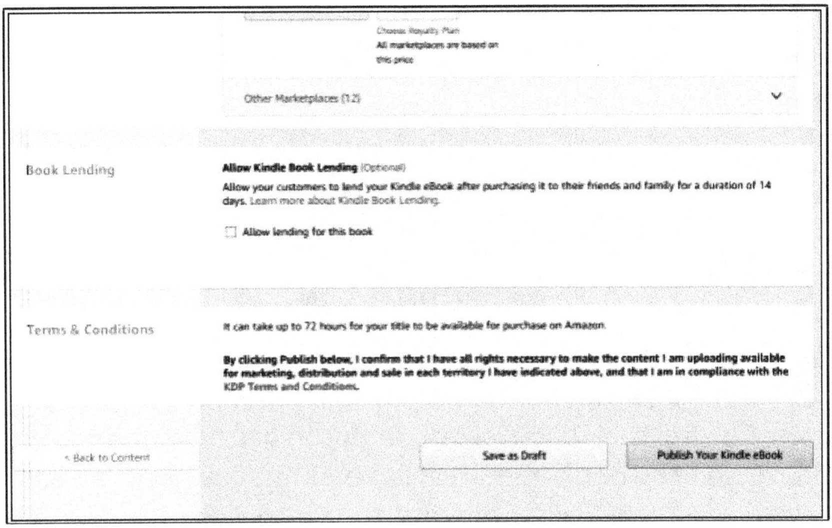

Figure 5: Publishing Kindle eBook on Amazon site

ADVANCED TRAINING

INTRODUCTION

Anything worth doing is worth doing well, do not just publish book when it is not well articulated. Authors should ensure that their work is published maintaining high standard and the book should also be of high quality. We should bear it in mind that our work would be online which means it will reach every town and village across the globe. There is a popular saying that the way you dress is the way you are addressed which means people will assess you and your book right from cover page, contents up to back cover. Authors and publishers should give proper attention to each and every aspect of book writing and publishing. You have the option to hire professionals to handle the organisation and publishing of your book and if you intend to handle every aspect of it by yourself, you have to upgrade your book publishing training from basic level to advance level. Publishing high quality books on Amazon site will attract readers to your work and you can earn cool money.

This section will teach you about Kindle Direct Publishing app called "Kindle Create" to format the manuscript of your book in order to organise the content properly, create attractive cover page that will draw readers' attention to your book and finally publish it as eBook and paperback. The training has been simplified to make the task easy for intending publisher, just follow the step-by-step procedure ad become self-publisher and earn from your published books.

TRAINING REQUIREMENTS

Publishers will need the following hardware and software to be successful in publishing their books on amazon site:

i. Computer system: You will need a good computer system or laptop that is internet ready.

ii. Good internet connection/wifi: This is necessary to download the appropriate software and complete the training online

iii. Kindle Create App: The application software is required for the advanced training and it is downloadable on the internet

Downloading and installing Kindle Create

Your computer system should be working on 64bits windows as operating system and click https://www.amazon.com/gp/css/homepage.html?ref_=nav_youraccount_btn to download Kindle Create software on Amazon website. Download the software and install on the computer system.

Double click the Kindle Create icon on the desktop to launch the software (figure 6)

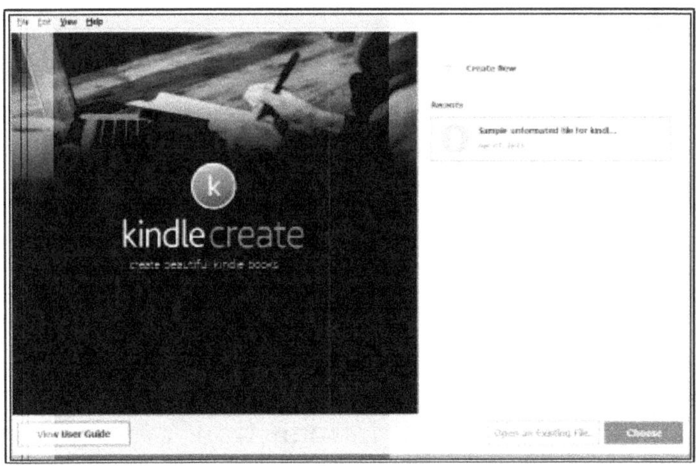

Figure 6: Kindle Create Interface

Open a new project from File menu and choose the manuscript

of the book prepared in Microsoft word. The manuscript will be loaded in Kindle Create for formatting.

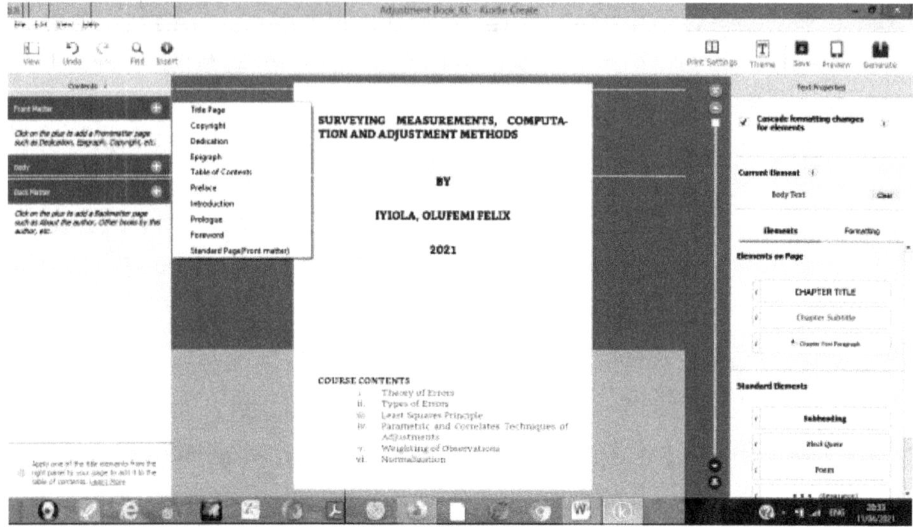

Figure 7: The main menu

The main menu comprises of three sections namely fron matter, body and back matter

Front Matter: This allows publishers to format the following pages:

    i.   Title page: you will be allowed to enter book title, sub-title, author's name, publisher and logo

    ii.   Copyright page: to supply information on copyright owner, year of publication and rights

    iii.   Dedication page: for dedication information

    iv.   Epigraph: for epigraph and attribution

    v.   Table of Contents: KDP app can be helpful to create table of contents for publishers

    vi.   Other vital information publishers can supply include preface, introduction, prologue and foreword

Body: This section allows publishers to format the content of the book, you can create pages and chapters with this option

Back matter: What you can do here include:

i. About the author: Author's biography can be supplied here
ii. Acknowledgement and other vital information can be included too

Printer settings: This is required to set the way headers and page numbers should appear in the book

Theme: This controls how elements will appear in the book and there are four options here namely Modern, Classic, Cosmos and Amour

Save: to save the work in kindle

Preview: This is to enable publisher view what readers will see on different devices

Generate: This will allow publisher to create book publishable in Kindle and on Amazon websites. This product can be open in KDP for further processing before final publishing

PUBLISHING EBOOK AND PAPERBACK IN KDP

L og into your Kindle Direct Publishing (KDP) account to print the formatted manuscript as either eBook, paperback or both.

Click Bookshelf and click paperback to display Paperback Details, Paperback Content and Paperback Rights and Pricing

Paperback Details: fill all the options like:

i.   Language: Select the primary language in which the book was written and by default "English"

ii. Book Title and subtitle: Enter the book title which cannot be edited after you might have generated ISBN for it

iii.Series: add series details if the book is part of a series

iv. Edition number: add edition number in digit like 1, 2, 3, …

v. Author: Add full name of the primary author

vi. Other Contributor: There is provision to add other authors to the book

vii.   Book description: Description of the book is very important and this will enable readers to have insights of the book to decide that the book is relevant to their work

viii.   Publishing right: This describes your publishing right to the contents of the book. It can be individual right or public domain work

ix. Keywords: Add up to seven (7) keywords to the book. This is necessary for readers to search and get your work

x. Fill categories and adult contents appropriately

Click Save and Continue to move to the next stage

Follow the steps described in Basic training for Paperback Content and Paperback Rights and Pricing and finally publish the book

EPILOGUE

It is certain that you have gained practical experience by following the steps in this training manual. It will go a long way to making positive change in your publishing life. This is the starting point and you lave laid a solid and strong foundation, continue to improve on what you have learned

ACKNOWLEDGEMENT

I use this medium to express my sincere gratitude to Mrs . Yemisi Okunnuga who taught me basic training on Amazon site. I also thank Ogapatapat who handled advanced training for publishing using Kindle Direct Publishing (KDP)

ABOUT THE AUTHOR

O. F. Iyiola

He is an academic staff at Federal School of Surveying, oyo and has taught and supervised both undergraduate and postgraduate students in the school. He holds M.Sc, in Surveying and Geoinformatics with specialization in Remote Sensing and Geographic Information System (GIS)